HOW TO
FLIP YOUR
FINANCIAL
FUTURE

DOUG ADDISON

How to Flip Your Financial Future
By Doug Addison

Printed in USA by
InLight Connection
PO Box 7049
Santa Maria, CA 93456

For ordering information contact:
InLight Connection
(800) 507-7853
To order: http://www.DougAddison.com

Cover Design by Christian Wetzel

Book design by
Treasure Image & Publishing
TreasureImagePublishing.com
248.403.8046

Contents

PART ONE

HOW TO FLIP YOUR FINANCIAL FUTURE

INTRODUCTION

In this book, I am going to be teaching about the Kingdom of God and what God has shown me concerning Biblical principles about finances.

Now whether you are a Christian or not, if you picked up this book I know you are going to be able to apply these principles to your financial plan because I am going to approach the subject in a very practical way.

It may be that you are new to understanding finances, you have just started taking some steps, or you are working your plan and seeing results. Perhaps you have even made significant breakthrough.

Wherever you are in your financial journey, I believe that the keys in this book will be valuable tools for your success.

You will learn:

- how to get out of debt

- practical strategies to increase your finances

- how to develop extra income through the Internet, (that is one of my specialties)

- business startup ideas

- developing non-profit strategies

- developing for-profit strategies to fund non-profits (This is really cool. It is something that is needed right now: Internet strategies to grow your business or ministry).

Doug's Journey

Let me begin by sharing some of my background information, just so you know my journey and what I have gone through. I was in banking and corporate management for a number of years and I was a business owner after that. Additionally, I was a consultant, computer network engineer, Life Coach, church planter and more.

I have learned a lot over my fifty-six years that I will be giving to you in the course of sharing my journey about what God has taught me. You can believe what you believe of course, but really, I think there is some good stuff that you are going to get out of this.

In 1987, I got off drugs and had a radical encounter with Jesus. Immediately after that, in 1988 God gave me an amazing job, which I worked until 1994 when I left and started a business. I sold that business in 1998. The purpose of my business was to free my time up so I could get ministry training.

I did not realize it at the time, but in that business God was preparing me for my present ministry, InLight Connection, which I have been doing for a number of years.

What Do You Want?

In this book, I am not going to be giving financial advice. This is also not a "wealth and prosperity" or a "name it and claim it" message. Rather, it is teaching about how to position yourself to have financial resources. There is a way to do it. There are things that you can do to position yourself to open the Heavens over you to fulfill what it is that God has called you to do.

Here is my saying and you can quote me:

"Prosperity is having the money, resources and freedom to do what God calls you to do, when He calls you to do it."

I do not know about you, but that is prosperity to me and I want that. I want the freedom. I am in this for the freedom to be able to do what God calls me to do when He calls me to do it, and that means I will need money to do it at times, and so will you!

So what about you? What do you want? Do you want more money? Maybe you want to pay off bills? Do you want to do something more practical, like fund your retirement, buy a house, a new car, or go to school? Do you want more money to give, maybe to charities, or to people in need? Maybe you want to start something that would help people in your community?

You may be the one who likes to give and give and give. Or like I mentioned in my journey, you may want to have more money to free up your time so that you can do the things that God calls you to do, in other words, the things that bring you life. Whatever it is, we are going to have a breakthrough.

Wisdom is Needed

Let's start by looking at some things first that can hurt you. Did you know that 80% of lottery winners actually lose it all within five years? That should sound an alarm. Most people are not even remotely prepared to deal with what we call the "sudden wealth syndrome."

Pride and greed can be intoxicating, so we need a strong foundation to build our financial future on. That is possibly why God is not blessing you yet. He wants to make sure you are not like one of those lottery winners. So that someday, when your prayers are answered but all hell also breaks loose over you, you will be able to handle it. It is God's great love and mercy protecting you.

He wants you to use wisdom, so in this book I am going to be talking a lot about wisdom. It is a Biblical financial message.

I think in the past people have focused their teaching on tithing, giving, and sowing in order to reap, but I want to focus more on the balance of this.

Now, these really are true statements. We do need to learn to discern when to give and what to give. Giving is the root or the foundation of it all, but you will learn it is not just giving your money.

"Humble yourselves, therefore, under God's mighty hand, that he may lift you up in due time." 1 Peter 5:6

We must have a spirit of humility. God will use money more than anything else to strengthen your faith, to test your motives and to guide you along.

It is usually money that will reveal our hearts, so humility is a big deal. In the business world (outside of religious circles), humility is not taught but it is something that we need to get a hold of.

THE PRINCIPLE OF GIVING

Biblical Principles of Giving

If you have been in churches, one of the most popular Bible verses you will hear used during the offering time can be found in the book of Luke:

"Give, and it will be given to you. A good measure, pressed down, shaken together and running over, will be poured into your lap. For with the measure you use, it will be measured to you." Luke 6:38

This is a true statement but if you look at the context of that verse, it is talking about judging others. Jesus said it was about forgiving others, but it still works with money, because that is what Biblical principles are.

The more you sow, the more you reap (2 Corinthians 9:6-7). Those that give will receive (Luke 6:38). If you humble yourself, you will be lifted up (1 Peter 5:6).

These are Biblical principles that work, no matter who uses them and you will find them all over the place.

"Bring the whole tithe into the storehouse, that there may be food in my house. Test me in this," says the Lord Almighty, *"and see if I will not throw open the floodgates of heaven and pour out so much blessing that there will not be room enough to store it."* Malachi 3:10

The reason that I developed this material is because many people have been bringing their tithe and they have been giving yet they have not seen the floodgates of Heaven open up. But I have. I have begun to see it and I want to help you. Did you know that there are some things that can clog up the release that has been promised?

There are some misunderstandings that are going around right now that need to be corrected. The bottom line is that we do need to give. Yes, it is about giving. Do you know what though? If you do not like to give, then do not do it.

"So let each one give as he purposes in his heart, not grudgingly or of necessity; for God loves a cheerful giver."
2 Corinthians 9:7 NKJV

This is so important. If you are upset about giving, do not give. But understand if you do that, if you develop that lifestyle of not giving, you are probably going to limit your financial future.

Give Extravagantly

I believe that we need to give extravagantly. The question is often asked, "Should we give 10% or not?" You know what? In the early church, people actually gave beyond their means. They were known for giving. This is what the apostle Paul was talking about, and people gave a lot.

"Remember this: Whoever sows sparingly will also reap sparingly, and whoever sows generously will also reap generously." 2 Corinthians 9:6

Some people need to learn to give. Other people need to learn to discern when to give and if they give too much, they need boundaries. We need to learn when to give, when not to give and to know what God is doing. I have been a giver all my life because my mom taught me to give.

However, because of that, I have actually given too much at times and I have had to use boundaries to bring it back to proper balance.

Change Your Mindset

As we move into this new thing, we really have to change our mindsets. When I came out of the darkness back in the 1980s, God gave me a promise through my sister. He appeared to my sister and told her to tell me that God would bless everything I put my hands to (quoting Deuteronomy 28:8). It was kind of like that. So I did not have to work hard. It was easy for me to make money before I was in ministry, when I was working in my business.

When God first called me to start making money for Kingdom purposes, once I got into ministry, it was really hard because a lot of people judged me. You have to have your heart in the right place, but God still wants us to have money.

I read in a book Dave Ramsey recommended, written by Jewish Rabbi Daniel Lapin, where he said, "What I do not understand about you Christians is not the Messiah; it is the fact that you have poverty." He said that as Jews, they believe that finances are worship. Traditionally, Jewish people do not have a problem with the power to get wealth.

However, as Christians we often feel guilty about making money. We need to break off guilt about prosperity and break off that limiting mindset. We need to go beyond "just getting by." It seems like we have a "getting by mentality." Instead of simply getting by, we need to get to the place where we can help supply the needs of other people, finance the works of God, including ministries and missions, while caring for our own families.

My wife Linda and I are in a position now where we can actually give our daughter and family money without asking for it back. That is where I have always wanted to be, especially as a grandfather. We learned how to develop streams of income to give back into the Kingdom.

FINANCIAL HEALING

Take a minute and think about what you want to get out of reading this book. Do you want to learn more about the Bible and what it says about finances? Do you want to get out of debt? Do you want to learn how to make extra money or get a financial breakthrough? Maybe all of the above? This book is going to cover all these things and more.

Getting Healed of Money Issues

To positively influence the world, it really takes a mindset change. I call it "Financial Healing." Getting healed of our money issues will require a mindset change for many people.

We have got to get rid of greed and the tightwad-miser attitude. Sometimes the issues are overspending or shopping addictions.

Generally, there is a great deal of misunderstanding about money.

"For the love of money is a root of all kinds of evil. Some people, eager for money, have wandered from the faith and pierced themselves with many griefs." 1 Timothy 6:10

This verse is often misquoted as, "Money is the root of all evil." However, it is not money itself that is the problem; it is the *love of money* that is greed and idolatry. If you can deal with that, then God can bring more money into your life. That is often why God will not give you all of the cash you need all at once. He wants you to press through to get your breakthrough.

We have to break through poverty mindsets and realize that with God all things are possible. My father was a coal miner in Virginia and I am not saying anything bad about him, but I had to break off a poverty mindset that I grew up with that caused me to feel guilty about finances. I felt guilty even for making money in ministry and tried to give it all away. I had to let go of the guilt that says we cannot serve God *and* have money.

The truth is, you cannot give it all away. Honestly, the people who think that everything should be free in ministry and churches are probably limiting their life and they will not get a breakthrough because their mindset is not even Biblical. We cannot have everything for free.

That is why Jesus had someone who handled the moneybag. Judas handled the money for Jesus' ministry. There were financial responsibilities even with Jesus' ministry.

We need to discover the healthy balance that God intended us to have regarding money, and then expand our possibilities and get creative so that we can change the world with God's love! That is why I love teaching about these breakthrough strategies.

God will test your motives. There will be seasons of lack and there will be seasons of plenty. These seasons are used to get you to press in and break through and also to show you what is in your heart. All things are possible for those who believe.

Do Not Settle for Less

We often settle for less, thinking we are being more spiritual. You know, when we over-spiritualize things, we will wrongly apply Biblical principles to our lives.

"But he said to me, 'My grace is sufficient for you, for my power is made perfect in weakness.' Therefore I will boast all the more gladly about my weaknesses, so that Christ's power may rest on me." 2 Corinthians 12:9

I have heard people say, "God's grace is sufficient for me, so it is okay, that is all I need."

However, when the apostle Paul said that, he was not talking about the context of money; he was talking about suffering and enduring persecution.

Yes, God's grace is sufficient! Absolutely! But we also need to break through poverty thinking and limiting mindsets to get a hold of creative

Kingdom financial strategies, especially in these days. Can we have wealth?

"Jesus answered, 'If you want to be perfect, go, sell your possessions and give to the poor, and you will have treasure in heaven. Then come, follow me.' When the young man heard this, he went away sad, because he had great wealth. Then Jesus said to his disciples, 'Truly I tell you, it is hard for someone who is rich to enter the kingdom of heaven.'" Matthew 19:21-23

Some people argue that we cannot have wealth because Jesus said in Matthew 19:23 that it is hard for a rich man to enter into the Kingdom of Heaven.

However, Jesus was not creating a doctrine by His statement. He was actually addressing an individual who had made money his god. Jesus never made that statement at any other time. The answer is yes, we can have wealth.

"May the Lord, the God of your ancestors, increase you a thousand times and bless you as he has promised!" Deuteronomy 1:11

Now listen, that is God's promise to you. He wants to increase you a thousand times and bless you. That is God's heart for us.

True Riches

Let's look at what true riches are because we need to define this.

"but lay up for yourselves treasures in heaven, where neither moth nor rust destroys and where thieves do not break in and steal. For where your treasure is, there your heart will be also." Matthew 6:20–21 NKJV

This is why God will test your heart. If we get our heart and motives in line with God's heart and purposes then we are able to handle wealth. A good Bible study for you would be a word search on riches. According to the Bible, *true riches* include wealth, but not just wealth; it is also revelation and wisdom and it is everything pertaining to the Kingdom of God.

FOUNDATIONS FOR A BREAKTHROUGH

Can You Handle Wealth?

First of all, God wants to make sure you can handle a financial breakthrough. If you can be trusted with earthly wealth then you can be trusted with Kingdom wealth.

"Whoever can be trusted with very little can also be trusted with much, and whoever is dishonest with very little will also be dishonest with much. So if you have not been trustworthy in handling worldly wealth, who will trust you with true riches? And if you have not been trustworthy with someone else's property, who will give you property of your own?" Luke 16:10–12

I love this verse! This is so important because God will use wealth on Earth to test you along the way. Whoever can be trusted with very little can also be trusted with much, and whoever is dishonest with very little will also be dishonest with much.

Be Fair and Honest

Here is the foundational breakthrough: you have got to be honest and fair.

The Bible has a lot to say about dishonesty, which of course is the opposite of honesty. There are abominations listed in the Bible that include many other things that some people are using to judge different people groups right now. They are using certain verses but did you know that *dishonesty* is mentioned as an abomination to God? We need to be fair and honest. I am not trying to bring guilt here; I am just trying to open people's eyes that honesty really does matter.

Jesus got angry at those who were money changers in the Temple in John 2:13-17. As a minister, I know I get accused all the time because I am charging for things; I have been called a "money changer."

But do you know what? Jesus was angry because the money changers were dishonest. It was not because they were using Kingdom financial strategies; they were ripping people off. They were manipulating their scales. It was called having dishonest scales.

"'Do not use dishonest standards when measuring length, weight or quantity. Use honest scales and honest weights, an honest ephah and an honest hin. I am the Lord your God, who brought you out of Egypt." Leviticus 19:35-36

Your Job Counts Now

So, here is a big one to get your breakthrough. This is how I got one of mine. God spoke to me one day that "your current job holds your breakthrough." I was crying out. I was screaming to God. (It is called intercession. Have you done it?) I was screaming to God one day and asking, "When are you going to free me of this?"

I was in my corporate job for a number of years. I felt called to something bigger, and I was getting some training. I was growing. It was 1993 and God spoke to me one day, "I will not release you until you realize that I placed you in this job."

And then he showed me Colossians 3:23-24:

"Whatever you do, work at it with all your heart, as working for the Lord, not for human masters, since you know that you will receive an inheritance from the Lord as a reward. It is the Lord Christ you are serving."

You will get an inheritance from the Lord for working with your "ungodly" boss. And that is what was happening with me. I was working in a job in San Francisco and it was a very, very hostile environment for me. Then God said, "It is not going to change until you realize this and start doing the very things that you do at your church at your job."

So I started praying and fasting for the company I worked for. I prayed for their finances and I started getting prophetic words and sharing them. Then they started noticing.

When it came time for me to leave my job and go off and get my ministry training and do things for the Kingdom, the reward came from them. They were the ones (not my church), who stepped up and said, "Wow, we see how you helped us." I got an inheritance, so to speak.

A year later they hired me back at five times the pay, but it was not until I understood that my job was my ministry that my breakthrough came. That is what you need to do. This is going to be one of the keys to your breakthrough right now.

There is Power in Being Content and Grateful

There is also power in being content right now, especially as prophetic people. We tend to live in the future.

"I know what it is to be in need, and I know what it is to have plenty. I have learned the secret of being content in any and every situation, whether well fed or hungry, whether living in plenty or in want. I can do everything through him who gives me strength." Philippians 4:12–13

People are very familiar with the portion of the verse that says, "*I can do everything through Christ who gives me strength.*" But if you look at the whole verse, it is actually in the context of being content. And so we can do everything through Christ who gives us strength, but it is in the context of being grateful for what you have right now.

Ask for More and Take Steps

Here is another breakthrough step. I teach this in my *Activate your Life Calling* course and to my coaching groups all the time. It is one of my main breakthrough strategies:

"*Ask, and it will be given to you; seek, and you will find; knock, and it will be opened to you. For everyone who asks receives, and he who seeks finds, and to him who knocks it will be opened.*" Matthew 7:7–8 NKJV

Now notice, A-S-K: **A**sk, **S**eek, and **K**nock. It is an acronym (ASK); and each of these are proactive steps. It does not say to sit on the couch and wait for God to open the door, even though that is what we see a lot of people doing these days. Yes, there is value in waiting, but you could be doing things now to prepare you for later. For example, there are people waiting for a job, waiting for a knock on the door. "*Knock Knock. Who's there? It is a job!*" It does not usually happen that way. You actually have to ask, seek, and knock and then things will be opened. Waiting on the Lord is biblical and powerful (Isaiah 40:31), but if you have not done the last thing He told you to do, start with that. Make sure you have done that last thing before you go into a season of waiting. Look for proactive steps to take to get your breakthrough.

Practical Things We Can All Do Regarding Finances

There are practical things that you can do. Here are a few tips I have learned along the way:

- Be wise and get advice, especially on big decisions.

- Learn to recognize God's voice. God will guide you and speak to you about your money.

- Do not assume that if you get a prophetic word about financial blessing that it is a free ticket to be irresponsible.

  This is so important. I coach some people who actually go in debt because they got a prophetic word that there is going to be financial blessings forthcoming. You may have gotten a prophetic word regarding financial breakthrough, but many times you will get words from God to prepare you because everything is going to look opposite at first.

  In fact, you may struggle financially before you get the breakthrough.

  So a prophetic promise is not a free ticket to be irresponsible with your finances; instead you need to be all the more diligent and responsible.

- Learn to live within your means.

- Use a budget or spending plan.

- Pay off debt and develop savings.

- Develop a lifestyle of earning, giving, saving and spending in moderation as a way of preparing for bigger things.

   Every part of this is vital; earning, saving, spending and giving. When people are uncertain, they tend to retreat and only earn and save.

   However, if everybody were to stop spending right now it would cause people to lose their jobs!

   We cannot do that. For example, there are people pulling their money out of the market right now because they think it is going to crash, but doing that is going to make it crash.

   Unless God speaks specifically, we are not pulling our money out of the market right now. We are in this for the long haul. God has told me to plan for the long term.

- Update your resume and your skills.

   Here are some things that you can do right now. Update your resume and your skills. Get some training in your current job, or learn something new. If you are not getting promoted at work, find out why. Ask them what you can do to improve. I did that once. I took some classes and then I was able to advance. It may be that you need to change jobs.

- Do your best at your job so if it comes time to cut staff, they will not want to lose you.

FINANCIAL BREAKTHROUGH IN THE BIBLE

In this chapter, I just want to point out a few things from the Word of God that have changed my life.

Three of Jesus' closest friends, the disciples Peter, James, and John had a fishing business. They were not just fisherman; they had a business. Jesus gave them a strategy when He first met them on how to catch a boatload of fish. In fact, they got to sell the fish that day. They got blessed financially.

"When he (Jesus) had finished speaking, he said to Simon, 'Put out into deep water, and let down the nets for a catch.' Simon answered, 'Master, we've worked hard all night and haven't caught anything. But because you say so, I will let down the nets.' When they had done so, they caught such a large number of fish that their nets began to break." Luke 5:4-6

Peter said, "Master, we worked hard on it all night and have not caught anything." Almost like he wanted to say, "Hey, you are a carpenter and a teacher. What do you know about fishing?" But they listened, let down their nets and they caught such a huge amount of fish that their nets began to break.

You know it is usually in deep water where you are going to get things. Put out to **deep water**. It requires taking a risk; it requires faith; it requires listening to God. When Jesus gets in your boat, He will bless your life and business as well.

Instructions Come Through Dreams

I am an experienced dream interpreter. Here are some helpful instructions about dreams. Jacob, who later became Israel, got a dream from God. He was the father of the twelve tribes of Israel, including Joseph, the dream interpreter.

"In breeding season I once had a dream in which I looked up and saw that the male goats mating with the flock were streaked, speckled or spotted. The angel of God said to me in the dream, 'Jacob.'

"I answered, 'Here I am.'

"And he said, 'Look up and see that all the male goats mating with the flock are streaked, speckled or spotted, for I have seen all that Laban has been doing to you.'" Genesis 31:10–12

In this passage, Jacob received a dream from God about a financial strategy on how to profit over his father-in-law, Laban, who was ripping him off. He got this simple strategy. God used the rejects of the flock to multiply them more than Laban's and gain a huge profit.

God told him to ask his father-in-law for the spotted and speckled sheep and goats that Laban did not want. Jacob's flocks grew huge and got blessed mainly because he got instructions through dreams. God will use you to bless where you work, and in turn your employer can bless you.

Hearing God for Big Strategies

When we need to hear God for big strategies, dreams and prophetic gifts really help. Here is what Joseph told his "boss."

"It is just as I said to Pharaoh: God has shown Pharaoh what he is about to do. Seven years of great abundance are coming throughout the land of Egypt, but seven years of famine will follow them. Then all the abundance in Egypt will be forgotten, and the famine will ravage the land. The abundance in the land will not be remembered, because the famine that follows it will be so severe. The reason the dream was given to Pharaoh in two forms is that the matter has been firmly decided by God, and God will do it soon."

"And now let Pharaoh look for a discerning and wise man and put him in charge of the land of Egypt. Let Pharaoh appoint commissioners over the land to take a fifth of the harvest of Egypt during the seven years of abundance. They should collect all the food of these good years that are coming and store up the grain under the authority of Pharaoh, to be kept in the cities for food. This food should be held in reserve for the country, to be used during the seven years of famine that will come upon

Egypt, so that the country may not be ruined by the famine." Genesis 41:28-36

Pharaoh had two dreams in Genesis 41 that Joseph interpreted.

Remember, Joseph is Jacob's son. If you go back to Genesis 31, at the time when God spoke to Jacob through the dream, Joseph was in Rachel's womb. This is significant. There was something about this new child being birthed that affected the father. That is what God is doing right now. Maybe you have heard about the "Joseph anointing." God is bringing this type of anointing to us again.

Joseph was in prison. Pharaoh had dreams that he did not understand, that troubled him. Then Pharaoh called for Joseph to interpret them and he gave the interpretation about seven years of feast coming and then seven years of famine. But Joseph not only interpreted the dreams, he stepped up and gave wisdom and advice on what to do and how to do it. He gave the Pharaoh a strategy. During that economic downturn they were blessed.

Likewise, you can be blessed. That is why I believe that God is doing this right now. I do not believe the negative reports from the naysayers. Please join me in not believing negative economic reports and prophecies circulating on the Internet.

During the big drought, there was a huge economic downturn and because Joseph listened to God, the whole family of Israel (Jacob) was blessed. They received new clothes, houses, gold, and huge amounts of blessing. God wants to use those *Josephs* and *Josephines* to bless the world right now and we need to get ready for that.

BREAKING OFF THE
SPIRIT OF POVERTY

At this point of the book, there is something that we need to address. Before we make true progress in our financial health, we must break off the spirit of poverty. I will start by sharing my experience with the spirit of poverty and generational poverty.

In 2002 I was working for John Paul Jackson as the National Dream Team Coordinator. Of course I was in the "dream interpretation mode" and I was learning a lot.

During that time, I had a dream. In my dream, a guy came up to me and started pulling out my teeth. I started bleeding and I was bleeding all over the place. I went from there and got into this red Porsche, and they were calling me "the rich doctor."

But as I got out of my car to go into my office, it was full of scalps. (Like in the Old West how Native Americans would scalp their enemies.) My office was full of bloody scalps all over the wall, and then everyone started calling me "the witch doctor" as opposed to "the rich doctor."

Now, there was more to the experience, but I woke up from that dream and was really puzzled. However, I knew it was something about my calling. I also knew it was something about wealth, because first I was called a *rich doctor,* but then there were things cutting that off because later in the dream I was accused of being a *witch doctor.*

Well, within a few weeks I was researching the generational calling on my mom's side of the family. Most of them had died from Huntington's disease, so we do not have a lot of information. I was just searching the Internet one day, and there it was – my mom's family tree! My goodness! There was a surviving great-granddaughter of my mom's uncle who had done a family tree. Through her research, we found out that about four generations ago in my family, my third great-grandfather was considered a witch doctor! He was Cherokee. They called him the doctor. He would pull teeth and bleed people for a living. And that was in my dream. Someone pulling my teeth, I was bleeding, and there were those Indian scalps – that is what was holding back my blessing.

Then we discovered that his father from the fifth generation back was Cherokee, living in Cherokee, North Carolina. He was a Christian, and very wealthy, but he had been chased off his land by the U.S. Government who wanted his gold. He was robbed. It was his son who was the witch doctor who really just took the gift the wrong way.

After learning this all within a couple weeks, Linda and I were sitting there and God told me, "There were generational curses from the negative four grandfathers. Pull forward the Cherokee blessing from five generations ago." And this is where I get my generational prophetic gifting.

So I did it and it was really simple. I just made a list of things and asked forgiveness on behalf of my family line. We prayed and broke off witchcraft and any connections. I named off all the different things that I could think of and prayed, "we ask forgiveness for that, and we pull forward those blessings from five generations ago – the wealth, the believing in Jesus, and the restoration in my family line." It took five minutes to do and God said this to me, "I want you to go to the store right now and buy thank-you cards for what is about to happen to you." And so we got in the car and went to the store. I went to get a desk, a cordless drill and the thank-you cards.

We put the thank-you cards and the cordless drill on the counter. The cordless drill rang up for $2.94. It was a $30 item. The clerk said, "We do not know why that happened, but you can have it for that price." Then we went over to Staples and bought a desk. It was a couple hundred-dollar desk and it rang up for $39, so we bought two!

Something shifted over my life that day in 2002. It is not like we got money dumped on us because we would not have been able to handle it, but something shifted in the Heavens over us, over me, and over my generational line at that point forward. It was not all at once. I still had to work through some things. But you have to understand that the losses, setbacks and sins in your generational past can really affect you.

Here is what you want to do. Make a list of things that you have seen repeated in your life, especially negative things. In my family it was poverty, divorce, alcoholism, even murder was in there. So we made that list and repented for anything that was not from God and called forward the opposite of all of those things. Make a list of the opposite virtues or strengths. The opposite of murder is life, or giving life. The opposite of poverty is wealth and giving wealth into the Kingdom. The opposite of witchcraft is the prophetic gifts and the gifts of the Spirit. Ask

God to bring forward in your life all the blessings and good things. I call this *pulling things forward.*

I want to pray right now and agree with you. Where two agree together it will be done. (Matthew 18:19)

Pray with me:

"God, we agree right now to break off all generational ties or negative connections to anybody's finances. But first I ask, God, that you would show us what Satan does not want us to see; just like you did in my family. Reveal those things that are not of you. And we call forward the blessings in the family line. We pull those things forward in the name of Jesus. Amen."

SOWING AND REAPING

Faith Actually Works

For many years there has been a faith message out there that has taught some spiritual principles that were designed by God. You will see spiritual principles applied all over the place; even the law of attraction works for people because it actually pertains to a principle from God about giving: what you sow you shall reap.

"Do not be deceived: God cannot be mocked. A man reaps what he sows ... Let us not become weary in doing good, for at the proper time we will reap a harvest if we do not give up." Galatians 6:7, 9

God responds to our faith and He wants to take care of our needs. This works for healing as well. We need to focus, but we also need a balance in this giving message. We can get so focused on the process of applying the principle that we let go of faith in God. Remember this: God will bless where your faith is.

Many people have misunderstood the message of giving, partly due to some of the abuse that has taken place out there to gain bigger offerings or whatever. In spite of all this, God is releasing new Kingdom, financial breakthroughs.

That message (many call it the "Word of Faith") is still active today. I just want to say that the Word of Faith leaders like Kenneth Hagin, Kenneth Copeland and Oral Roberts got a revelation from God and it was real. If you listen to their preaching or you get around them, they have a direct revelation that ignites faith for healing and giving.

The principles they taught still work and are from God, but they can be abused and sometimes misapplied. That is why I am careful not to focus on the offering too much in my meetings. But there are times when the anointing is there for it.

Do you have a giving story? God will give you one if you do not already have one. Ask Him to bless you in some way.

Here is what happened to me.

I have been a giver and a tither all my life, but even though I was generous, I noticed that we were still regularly in debt and struggled financially. God spoke to me and said it was my own offenses against others that kept me from understanding these amazing principles of reaping what I needed. Faith preacher offering messages turned me off. My own offense was keeping me from understanding and activating these principles in my life. I learned that our own beliefs and bad experiences can sometimes stand in the way of our financial breakthrough. This is also true for healing.

In 2010 we were $50,000 in debt, we had $1,000 in the bank, we were about to go under. Then God spoke to me that I did not understand the principles about seed and sowing. I turned on the TV to a Christian TV station and there was a minister saying those exact words, "Let me just share with you everything that God told me about seed and sowing." And it was the same guy that I had been offended by! I knew I had to listen to him and I needed to activate my faith.

I knew where he was going. I knew that there would be a $1,000 offering at the end. But then God told me there had been two other times in the last few years that He had spoken to me that powerfully and I said no to it because it got to that $1,000 offering and I was offended by it.

So I decided to go with it. Linda and I gave $1,000 to a group that was doing what we wanted to do, which involved TV and the media. As part of the offering, they instructed us specifically to ask God for what we needed, so we specifically asked God for debt reduction and a BMW to do the things He called us to do in Hollywood. I am not into cars and material things, but we had to activate our faith. Then we had to go test-drive the

BMW. When we did, we had an encounter with the salesman. I interpreted his dream and it blessed him so much. I prayed for his entire family and it was an amazing time.

Then we got really clear on what we needed. This was the Word of Faith message that we needed to grab hold of. This is the process. Get clear on it. We printed it out and I put it in my Bible and on our refrigerator. We prayed over our needs and began to call those things in.

Check this out: I was ready to give the TV preacher $100 but God said he wanted to multiply it by ten. So ten times 100 is $1,000. We gave him $1,000. He multiplied that by ten! Ten months to the day after we gave that $1,000 someone gave us $10,000 plus more. There was more money but they told me, "God said that this is $10,000," and so we were able to buy a pre-owned BMW which has helped opened the door for us to start doing things in Hollywood, like prophesying to people in the arts and entertainment industry and taping in

Hollywood. Inspiration Network came out and did a story on us, Darren Wilson filmed us for the *Father of Lights* documentary and *The Tattoo Prophet* reality show also opened up right at that time. All because we took that time and activated our faith.

You may be saying, "Well, I am giving. Why am I not getting a breakthrough?"

Let's go back to that verse where Jesus said:

"Do not judge, and you will not be judged. Do not condemn, and you will not be condemned. Forgive, and you will be forgiven. Give, and it will be given to you. A good measure, pressed down, shaken together and running over, will be poured into your lap. For with the measure you use, it will be measured to you." Luke 6:37–38

As we saw before, many are familiar with verse 38, the one that says, *"Give, and it will be given to you. A good measure, pressed down, shaken together ..."* right? But look at the verse before it. This could be the very reason why you are not getting your breakthrough.

Jesus said, "*Do not judge and you will not be judged. Do not condemn and you will not be condemned. Forgive and you will be forgiven.*" (That is the ramp right there.) "*Give and it will be given to you. Good measure, pressed down, shaken together and running over, will poured into your lap. For with the measure you use, it will be measured to you.*"

Jesus was talking about forgiveness and judgment in this text. Remember it is a spiritual principle, so it works for anything—including your money.

Judgments against others can hold us back. I had a judgment against faith preachers. I had judgments against other people. I had a judgment even recently against a publishing company that had mistreated me and I had to forgive them. So we need to clear the spiritual atmosphere around us.

"*Therefore, if you are offering your gift at the altar and there remember that your brother or sister has something against you, leave your gift there in*

*front of the altar. First go and be reconciled to them;
then come and offer your gift.*" Matthew 5:23-24

We need to reconcile in our hearts and
reconcile with others when we can. I also
recommend going on a "negative talk fast." Just
abstain from all negative talk.

Finally, we need to give love, grace and
gratitude as well as money. This clears the spiritual
atmosphere and opens the heavens over us.

If you would like to read more about this, then
you can find blog posts on my website,
DougAddison.com. Just search "I'm not getting my
breakthrough" and the results should lead you to
the posts about this topic.

Taking Practical Steps

Having faith and confessing it with your
mouth is sometimes not enough. If you are not
seeing a breakthrough then you need to take
radical steps. Sometimes you need to ask, seek
and knock, (Matthew 7:7). You need to cleanse

your atmosphere. Are you getting focused prayer? What are some practical steps you can take now? Are you delaying doing something that God has instructed you to do?

For me, one of the other reasons I could not move forward with all this was because I had not followed through with what God had told me about launching the online *Dream Crash Course*. When I finally did so, everything else opened up right after that.

Pray with me:

"Father, we pray that you would open things up right now and that you would change the spiritual atmosphere around us and cause blessings to flow through. Show us where we have allowed offense to take hold in our hearts and attitudes. Give us grace to forgive and bless our enemies, and those who have hurt and disappointed us. Forgive us for judging others. Give us grace to see what we have been blind to. Amen."

GETTING OUT OF DEBT

The Debt Epidemic

There is a debt epidemic happening right now. Debt is a huge problem that is draining the life and future out of people everywhere. We need to break out of it.

"Let no debt remain outstanding, except the continuing debt to love one another, for whoever loves others has fulfilled the law." Romans 13:8

"The rich rule over the poor, and the borrower is slave to the lender." Proverbs 22:7

Here are some signs that debt might be controlling you:

- Living paycheck to paycheck: do you find yourself having no money immediately after you get paid?

- Creditors are calling: collection calls can ruin your day.

- Impulse spending: when you see something you want, do you immediately buy it?

- Money fights: to those who are married, this applies to you. Are you and your spouse fighting over money matters?

Here is what you need to do to reduce your spending and lower your debt:

- Be honest about your condition. Start a spending journal and keep track of everything you spend on a daily basis.

- Make financial goals. Set some realistic financial goals for yourself and your family. Try simple things like starting a vacation or Christmas savings account.

- Cut up the credit cards. Studies have shown that people spend a larger amount when using a credit card because it does not register that you are spending real money.

- Get an accountability partner. When you are trying to break any habit, it is important to surround yourself with people who have your back.

- If you do not have a plan that you are currently using, I have some good resources that I will be sharing with you later in this book. These are things that we used ourselves.

Here are some common myths about debt:

- "Debt is a tool for investing."

    My goodness, do not do it. Do not go into debt to invest. That is a terrible idea. Without a spending plan you can get in over your head quickly.

- "You need debt to build your credit."

    Well, actually, "building your credit" means you have to go into debt just to be able to get more debt in the future. You are better off building your savings.

- "Debt consolidation works."

    This is a lie. You might need it temporarily, but it will keep you in debt way longer.

Grow Your Savings

The best thing to do is to grow your savings account. You have to be willing to start small. Discipline is not learned overnight, so take small steps on a daily or weekly basis and you will start to see a different behavior forming. This is what is going to open things up.

You also have to prepare for emergencies. One of the great things about being a saver is that you have money put away for emergencies or unexpected events.

Once you discipline yourself to save money it will be easier to plan for big purchases like new furniture or a family vacation. Some people do a debt consolidation and then turn around and get right back in debt again.

If that is you, you need to get to the root of that. Stay out of debt and build wealth. You want to use the disciplines. With money in the bank you will be able to focus on paying off debts, investing, and helping others do the same.

Make Extra Income

This is so important. Do not be a victim. You have power to change and get a financial breakthrough. There are so many things you can do right now to make extra money, and then use the money towards debt reduction or your goals.

Later in this book, I am going to be talking about strategies on the Internet, working as a freelancer, picking up part-time side jobs, cleaning houses, babysitting or cooking. All of these are things that you can do to help others while earning extra money to reach your financial goals.

Radical Steps Get Radical Results

Here are some radical steps that I took. In 1993 I was in debt. I had a call to ministry and I took radical steps to be able to leave my corporate job in 1994.

Here is what happened in that one year. I downsized my life. I got out of my big car loan. I had a big van because I was using it as a youth leader, and instead I got a cheaper, older car. I got out of my big apartment and I house-sat and sofa-surfed for six months. Maybe you are not able to do that, but I was able to do that at my church.

Then I started a side business fixing computers. I was still working my corporate job. I traded time with others. I am not saying you have to do this, but where there is a will there is a way! What are some small or big steps you can take right now?

Dave Ramsey to the Rescue

What I just shared with you is what I did before I got married. After several years of marriage and planting new churches, my wife and I found ourselves in debt. Years later we went to Dave Ramsey's nine-week class called *Financial Peace University*. Thank God for Dave Ramsey! He has helped millions of people get out of debt and restore peace to their lives.

You can go to his website, DaveRamsey.com, and download his free eBook with budgeting tools. I recommend you read his book entitled *Total Money Makeover*, and take his *Financial Peace University* course. That is what we did.

We also helped others do the same. In his class, Dave Ramsey outlines seven "baby steps" to take to move from debt to building wealth.

- Baby Step 1: Put $1,000 in a beginner emergency fund

  The first thing is not to just start paying off everything. The first thing is to get a $1,000 emergency fund.

  That way, if something pops up in the future, you will not need to use your credit card. You are going to have the money in the bank.

- Baby Step 2: Pay off all debt with "the debt snowball"

  After baby step one is completed, it is time to start paying off your debts. Make a list of your debts from smallest to largest (except your mortgage). Pay off the smaller debts first and then the larger debts. He calls this the "snowball effect." You pay off one credit card, and then you roll that money you had been paying over into the next. You keep rolling it over and then it will pay down much faster.

- Baby Step 3: Fully funded Emergency Fund (3-6 Months of Expenses)

  When you are debt-free (excluding your house), go back to your emergency fund and build it for three to six months of expenses. That way, if you have an emergency like a major home repair, or job loss, you are prepared.

- Baby Step 4: Invest 15% Of Income Into Roth IRAs and Pre-Tax Retirement Plans

- Baby Step 5: College Funding

- Baby Step 6: Pay Off Your Home Early

- Baby Step 7: Build Wealth And Give

   After you have your emergency fund set, you can start your retirement plans, start your children's college funds, pay off your home early and start investing.

My wife and I got out of debt using this program. Now we are in step four. It has taken a few years but we were able to do it.

Be Encouraged

I want to say this: do not be discouraged.

"Jesus looked at them and said, 'With man this is impossible, but with God all things are possible.'" Matthew 19:26

Once you take steps towards getting out of debt or saving for the future then something positive happens in the spiritual realm. It takes time, but you can do it.

I want to pray for you right now:

"Father, for those who are in debt, I pray for a strategy from Heaven. God, I pray that you will open up their finances. I pray that you will open these things up. Let that extra income come in. I pray for inheritances that were not there. I also pray that you will break the root issues. Reveal to us any root issues that may be holding us back. And I pray for encouragement right now in Jesus' name. Amen."

STRATEGIES TO MAKE MORE MONEY

Once you start taking care of the debt and you get the plan into place, you are going to need a strategy to make more money.

Strategic New Season 2015-2022

On September 11, 2001, the United States got hit with terrorism. It was tragic. It brought fear into our society. Terrorism is fear. When people start operating in fear, they start holding back.

After a seven-year period, in September 2008, there was the largest bankruptcy in U.S. history and a major financial downturn in the housing market crash. People lost their homes—more fear. They lost their retirements and investments—more fear.

Seven years later is right now.

At the time of this writing, it is September 2015, and we are entering a new seven-year cycle. We are going to see a turnaround, even though many people do not believe it. Some people are saying it is another economic crash. No. It is not. God is going to do something new.

I tell you this: plan for the long-term, because we are going to do some new things right now.

For-Profit Strategies for Non-Profit Organizations

I am not saying that non-profit organizations are going to lose their tax-exempt donation status, but there are financial uncertainties and people are giving less right now. Things are tightening up. We may lose our tax shelter for donations from the government in the future so we will need creative financial strategies to survive if that does happen.

A non-profit church, ministry or organization might not be able to have a business of its own, but that does not mean you cannot start a for-profit business to fund non-profit work. The following are a couple of examples.

When I started my computer business in San Francisco, we also started planting churches. We were able to get the ministry up and running in the first year because I was a computer network engineer on the side. I was doing side jobs while I was planting a church, which funded that church. The business allowed us to rent a building, renovate it, and get up and running with 100 people within one year, because I had actually gotten blessed with my computer business.

Here is an example of a man that understood these principles. He was really into missions and he was not able to pay himself as a pastor, so he needed a way to fund the work he felt God calling him to do.

He noticed that on the west side of his city there were no burrito shops because of a high Asian population. He was one of the first ones to open a burrito shop in this area. It was so successful that he got to employ people from his church and even opened a second shop. He was able to fund all of his missions and pay himself as a pastor, because of a burrito shop!

I heard this story about another church that was close to Napa, California, where they make wine. They bought a vineyard and the people in the church began to grow and sell grapes to the wineries. It was so successful they were able to fund their ministry and building.

Welcome to the New Normal

Here is a prophetic word about the Internet that we really need to get a hold of. Because of what Bill Gates and Steve Jobs did for us with computers and the Internet, God spoke to me and said He is opening new **gates**, Heavenly gates, and He is providing **jobs** to people because of their (Bill Gates' and Steve Jobs') efforts. You really need to tap into this.

Welcome to the new normal:

- The largest hotel company in the world does not even own a hotel: AirBnb.com

- The largest retailer in the U.S. is now going around the world and does not even have a retail store: Amazon.com

- The largest taxi company in the world owns no taxis: Uber.com

Welcome to this new time and we can cash in on it.

Old versus new model for business:

It is a do-it-yourself world right now.

- Self-publishing has replaced traditional publishing.

- Funding used to be through small business associations and loans; now we can raise capital through kickstarter.com and gofundme.com

- With the old way you needed a degree; in the new way you need ambition and ideas.

- With the old way you needed to hire a consultant; in the new way you look on the Internet. There are coaches, articles, and lots of things that can help you get started.

- With the old way you had to have overhead and offices and staff. The new way is that you can work virtually; a virtual assistant can help you, and you can have minimal overhead.

- The old way meant marketing companies and expenses. The new way uses social networking and Internet websites.

I am not saying there is no value in some of the old things. For example, I still hire consultants when I need to. I still value the old, but I am operating in the new.

Starting a Business

A recent census bureau report said that over 60% of new business startups either had no capital at all or under $5,000. That is amazing! That means 26% did not even need capital.

Why are more people not doing it and cashing in? Fear and ignorance. Maybe they do not even know about it or maybe they do not know where to start.

So, I want to actually put you on the road to something that is going to help you; one of these new ways is freelancing.

Freelancing:

In the next five years, studies show that over 80% of the jobs being performed will be done in some way online. This might be things like telecommuting, online businesses or stay-at-home freelancers. There is a surge right now in working and making money online through the Internet.

You can prepare for this now. Anything that you can do that you are good at, you can actually do for someone else and get paid. It is similar to when some people take a pregnancy leave and they work part-time one day a week at home, you can also do this and make money at it.

Do not be fooled, it is hard work, but it gives you flexibility of time. Some people make it sound like you are going to have all this free time when you have an Internet business. It is a lot of hard work to get going, but it is not impossible.

Hiring a Freelancer:

God spoke to me about my ministry, InLight Connection, and we started five years ago to decentralize the staff. Now 80% of our team are freelancing contractors around the country. It has taken us a few years to get the bugs out and it is working for us. We still have an office; we have a bookkeeper who does a great job at our office and a shipping person. We use GoToMyPC.com and we use all kinds of different tools online to function efficiently long-distance.

There is a difference between a contractor and an employee. An employee comes to your office and you tell them when they are going to be working and you provide the computers or the desks.

A freelancer or a contractor provides their own equipment. You cannot do this just to try to save money on taxes; you have got to be honest so that you do not get in trouble for this.

The downside of hiring contractors is they can actually choose their own hours. But we work with a lot of people that work different schedules and it works out. They know when we need them. It just seems to flow.

Online business ideas:

Here are some online-business ideas that I want to share with you.

- Virtual Assistant:
  A virtual assistant is someone who works out of their home and helps people with different things like

bookkeeping, scheduling and assisting with events, calendaring, all types of things.

I have virtual assistants that work with me. I also use fancyhands.com. I have been using them for years. They do many things and I pay a fee for tasks performed.

If you want to become a virtual assistant I recommend visiting websites like zirtual.com or eahelp.com and finding out the criteria to be listed as a virtual assistant.

Do some research and contact your local businesses; maybe there are people in your church that would need this kind of assistance. You do not have to be very far away. You can be across town and be a virtual assistant.

- Blogger:

     You can make money blogging, which I talk about in my *"Write Your Book Now!"* online course.

- Transcription service, proofreading, writing or editing:

    This is in high demand now, and these are services that we use in the ministry.

- Freelance or project work through websites like Upwork.com or Fiverr.com:

    Fiverr.com is a website where service providers offer their services for as low as $5. Yes, you can actually make a lot of money from Fiverr on the side. Not all tasks are only $5.

    They allow you to offer upselling services to the base fee of $5. This will enable you to pay your debt off sooner or invest more into the Kingdom.

- Develop an eCourse:

    I started doing this years ago and it helps take your message to the world.

    Unlike coaching or consulting, you can record it once and sell it over and over which gives you a greater reach.

- Social media consultant:

    This is helping people develop or grow Facebook and Twitter followers by managing their social media posts and interactions.

- Web design or support:

    This service is helping a person or company build, design and maintain their website. It can also be customer support for their products and services.

- Resume/cover letter writing:

    In my first business years ago, I wrote resumes.

- Life or spiritual coach, health or nutrition coach:

    People are hiring coaches with all kinds of expertise these days.

- Internet marketing:

    This is a specialized field to help people learn to promote and sell their products or services online.

- eBook author

- Remote technical support

- Sell items on eBay or used books on Amazon.com

As you can see, there are many things that you can do to start a business and generate income.

Tips for Starting a Business or Ministry

- Do your research:

    Remember that just because God spoke to you to do something does not guarantee success. Find someone doing what you want to do and study how they do it. Read their books and talk to them. Most people who are successful actually help "hungry" people. They will answer your questions.

- Start small:

    Do not be afraid to start out really small. Do not try to be perfect. Just do it.

Do not be discouraged by humble beginnings or compare yourself to the big companies who have taken years to perfect their process or website. Just start out right now any way you can.

- Consider starting online:

    This is what I have been stressing because there is low overhead and a lot of people out there who might benefit from what you have. You only need to find a few to succeed.

- Things you can do in person:

    Starting your own business is not limited to the Internet. There are so many services that you can offer including pet care, housecleaning, yard work, repairs, computer help, etc.

    You could run errands, shop and cook for people, plan parties, organize and schedule appointments. There are tons of options. In fact, I am always looking for help in these areas.

You do not have to work online, but I highly recommend if you run an in-person business that you market yourself online.

Ideas to Market Your Small Business

There are many online resources for small businesses and service providers. Websites like craigslist.org and AngiesList.com are familiar to most people. TaskRabbit.com and Thumbtack.com are two up-and-coming sites. I hire people off Thumbtack.com all the time.

If I want a task done or something fixed, they can come over and do it. You can also hit the streets and put some flyers in local stores. Many businesses offer community bulletin boards for you to post flyers or business cards.

Find other businesses doing what you want to do and team up with them. This is how I started out with my computer business. I went to my tax consultant and said, "I am starting this new computer business. I will do some computer work for you at a reduced rate if you would refer me to some of your clients."

Then I made a little flyer and made it easy for him and he included it in his mailings. I developed more and more clients that way by networking with other businesses. I worked cheaper for him at first to get going.

Later I raised my rates as my business got established. Doing things together is what it is all about.

GROW YOUR BUSINESS OR MINISTRY ONLINE

Simple Online Strategy

If you do not get anything else out of this book, what I am going to share with you in this chapter is worth more than the price of this book. This is what we have been doing. I invested thousands to learn this.

These are simple strategies.

- Have a good website like WordPress, Wix, or Weebly

    First of all, have a good website. Do not invest too much to start. We have a WordPress website and our website has progressed over the years. If you do not know where to start, Wix.com or Weebly.com are a couple that are practically free to start out. But get something out there.

Do not invest in a $5,000 website up front. When you are ready, check out our current website: DougAddison.com. We put $5,000 into that, but that was after a number of years and we worked our way up to it. It also works on an iPhone. But I want to tell you this: we started out on a free template. We started out on something similar to the Wix.com site and worked our way up.

- Collect email addresses of visitors with an opt-in box:

  The next step in growing an online business is to collect the email addresses of your visitors. If you look at DougAddison.com, the first thing you see at the top of the page is a link that says "Download my free eBook" where visitors submit their email address to download the book.

  It is at the top and right up there in the design where my designers did not want me to put it. But I knew that growing my list was so important that we needed it to be visible. This allows our visitors to opt-in for my ministry announcements and offers. You have to collect these email addresses so that you can later engage with them. It is similar to having people come into a store and leaving their business card or signing up for a newsletter.

Your email list is your biggest asset ever. That is why you will want to collect those email addresses, because when you start doing events, writing things, and offering products, you are going to want to let people know about it.

• Use an autoresponder program to automate a personal connection with customers, such as MailChimp, Aweber or Constant Contact:

Some are free, some are not. Some are only $25, so they are very affordable. It is really important to have an automated response so that you can create a series of automatic email responses and be able to develop a relationship with people and introduce yourself to them. This is very important.

- Offer a free download or eBook (this is a must):

  No longer do people want your newsletter. If you have "Sign up for my free newsletter" on your website, you need to find a way to give them a free product that will benefit them. My email list was at 5,000 subscribers just a few of years ago and it was less than two years ago when we put that free eBook on our website. Our email list went from 5,000 to 50,000 in 18 months primarily from that free eBook. It exploded because people want something of value.

- Stay in touch with a monthly update (e-newsletter):

  In other words, do not ignore your list. Send out regular e-updates. This is a great strategy, and you have to do this.

- Use social media to connect with existing and new followers.

  Facebook, Instagram and Twitter are a must.

- Blog, blog, blog!
    You have got to blog. You have got to stay in touch with your audience in some way.

- Develop online services or products:
    Develop online services or products on top of all you are doing. This might be recorded messages they can download, eBooks, coaching, or online courses.

This is the online strategy that God gave me and we use it. For me it is not about making money, it is more about getting my messages out to the world. But it takes money to do that. Walt Disney said, "We do not make movies to make money, we make money to make more movies."

Do not spend a lot of money on startup costs, and do not compare yourself to the big ones. Start now. If you do not have much cash, get a free Wix account, then go over to Fiverr.com and you can pay someone $5-$500 to give you a web design on your Wix account. As you can see, there is something for every budget.

Create a Digital Product

You will want to create a digital product. This is so important because people want you to help them with answers to their questions. They want a problem solved, they want to relieve their pain or save time and money. Those are the things that will get them. People will pay money for those things.

I know I do! If I need a problem solved, I will start researching online. If I see someone's eBook, I will pay for it. If it is something that is going to help me, I will buy it. Those digital products that you can create can be available at any time. It can be an eBook, a report, an audio, video, or something of value.

Yes, it is okay to charge for some of these things. How can a $1-$5 digital download be powerful? Once you create it, there are no more expenses. You offer it over and over. What if someone downloads a digital product?

For example, we had a few of the smaller products for sale. They were Kindle books that retail from $0.99 to $2.99. We market them and we blog about them, and we are receiving several hundred dollars a month for doing very little. It is autopilot income. That is what you want to do.

Writing a Book

I really encourage people to write a book. I have an online course called *Write Your Book Now!* It is a great resource that gives you everything you need to get your book done. You can find out more about that in the resource section of this book, and I highly recommend it to anyone with a goal or dream to write a book. There has never been a time like this to do it. Kindle Direct Publishing makes it so easy to self-publish nowadays.

You can still write a book the old way. Let's say you have a core message that you want to get out there. Maybe it is about how to rescue dogs or help children in some way; or how to help people discover their destiny. You can go to a publisher. It is going to take over a year and they will actually pay for most of the publishing process for you, but you only get about 15 percent back in royalties.

Most people think that they are going to get rich off of book royalties. They really have a big surprise coming when they go to their mailbox, because it really is more of an investment to publish a book. This is different for those who are fortunate enough to write a bestseller. You have better odds of getting struck by lightning on the same day that you won the lottery.

Keep in mind that publishing your book through a traditional publisher may get your name out there and it is almost like advertising, but it is not always going to help you.

Let's look at a quick example. Say that your publisher sells 1,000 of your books in a year. Your book retails for ten dollars each and the publisher gives you a 15 percent royalty. That is $1,500 a year. (Not a lot.) Now let's say *you* sell 1,000 copies of the book yourself. The publisher will typically sell your book to you at a 50-60 percent discount, so they are charging you five dollars per book. If you sell 1,000 books yourself at ten dollars each you will net $5,000. These are very average, really honest, and maybe even generous numbers. You would make $6,500 (or $541 a month) minus any expenses that you have, but the publisher owns the rights to your book. That means that you are limited in what you can do with the message. You have to be careful and read your contract closely.

Here is the new writing strategy God gave me. This was one of the things that we were able to do to get my ministry out of debt and to reduce my travel schedule, which was grueling. Right now itinerant speakers who are using the old speaking model have to be out there doing 20 events a year at least. That kind of schedule wears on you over time.

Here is the new strategy God gave me. Let's say you have your core message. Before you write your book, create an online course. You upload it to your website once. Let's just say it is five online sessions. You record a video or even create an audio download (MP3) and a PDF workbook. These can be made right on your word processor; and the whole process is relatively inexpensive to get up and going. You can record the sessions directly from most computers. You can also hire virtual assistants to help you with editing or formatting of the workbook if you need it.

Let's say you offer it for $50. That is very fair. It comes to ten dollars a session. Let's say you sell 1,000 of those. That is $50,000. Then you create three more audio downloads (MP3s) on that same message and you sell them for $5 each. That is a very fair price for an audio download. They could be recordings from where you spoke at an event or at a church, or you can record them right in your own home office. If you sell 1,000 of these new MP3s, you have just generated another $15,000.

That would give you $65,000 for your first year. That is about $5,400 a month, minus expenses. WOW! That is way more than the $500 from the traditional publishing model. And the bonus is that *you now own your message*. You can do anything you want with it like create a study guide or break it into smaller eBooks.

If you create your online course first, then you have the capital to hire people to help you self-publish it into a book. You have a built-in audience, because you have this online group who has been taking it. You have 1,000 people in there who are excited and they probably have 1,000 friends who are excited and ready for your book! You can choose to convert those online sessions into a book. You can have someone help you with that and self-publish it.

Now you have over $50,000 in the bank to actually invest in a book launch. Most of the time when you go to a publisher you do not have money. The book comes out and then they give you the name of a publicist. It is at least $5,000 to work with a publicist. Oftentimes, you do not have the money because you have not sold a single book yet! If you use this new God-given strategy that I have been sharing, you will have money in the bank and a built-in audience.

Here is what I did with my book, "*Understand Your Dreams Now.*" Remember I said that God would not move me forward until I did something about the *Dream Crash Course* in 2010?

I wrote the *Dream Crash Course* and released it at a low price because I wanted to build a following for the message. I raised the price over time, but it was still under ten dollars per session (for ten sessions).

The course covers everything you need to interpret dreams. Everyone who has taken the course has been thrilled with it and we have sold a lot. Everywhere I go people want me to interpret their dreams or do some dream training. I encourage them to take the *Dream Crash Course* first so that by the time I come back to train them, we can all be at another level. It has really helped us out.

Again, this is not just about making money. It is about getting our messages or services out to the world. Some people judge me for doing this in a ministry. Most people who think everything in the Kingdom should be free are probably struggling with debt and not fulfilling their destinies.

I released the *Dream Crash Course* online in 2010 and in 2013 I converted it to a book. I actually had the ten sessions and I have a little bit more than ten chapters. Everyone has been excited about it. The best part is we had the finances in the bank to pay for the book publishing and some promotional expenses. This is a new writing strategy. Because I own the rights to the material, we can pick one chapter and sell it on Kindle or in a smaller eBook. You can do this too. You can also develop a coaching program based on your message. You are now able to take your message to the world in a variety of forms.

Becoming a Coach

You can become a coach. It is an up and coming online career. You can do it part-time or you can build it into a business but it is great to start part-time. There are many different types of coaches.

The one that is the most popular is a life coach or a productivity coach. They help you stay on track with what you are called to do.

When I first started out in 2005, I hired a life coach to help me stay on track and then I actually became a coach myself. Coaches usually work over the phone or through Skype. They basically help you with self-discovery. Just like in sports, the coaches do not know more than the athlete, but they are able to provide an outside vision for the athlete to move them into their full potential.

I have tried all kinds of coaches and I have found my niche. I am a prophetic life coach, because I have found out that I am really good at doing things in a short period of time. I am not as good on the longer pastoral-type of relationships where we are meeting all the time. I am much better at helping people get a breakthrough in a short period of time. So, I developed a strategy for prophetic life coaching and it works for me.

Some people judge me for what I charge, but I want to tell you that God gave me this strategy. I tried charging less for it, but the wrong types of people came who were not ready for a breakthrough, and it made it a less successful experience for me and for them. I can help people get a breakthrough in 30 minutes. I can unleash the prophetic, use my coaching skills, then bring people back around, and we can break things off quickly. Things can be done in 30-40 minutes.

I am not saying that I cater more to people who can pay more, but there is something about people who are hungry. When you are hungry, you are ready. Coaching also keeps me off the road. When I do prophetic life coaching, it actually brings money into my ministry and it allows me to stay home from traveling on the weekends. The amount that I would normally make on the road, I can make with coaching, and I can do it throughout the month from my office. So, for me and my clients, coaching is great. I love coaching.

Activate Your Life Calling

Coaching is great, but lasting change usually happens over time as we learn to change our behavior and develop new patterns. God gave me this strategy to develop *Activate Your Life Calling*, which is a strategic three-month online breakthrough experience.

I am telling you this because this was part of my process to go from writing my book, *Personal Development God's Way*, to doing my prophetic life coaching in the 30-minute life sessions. Then I thought, "Wow, God showed me that we need this three-month period because it takes time to move into a new season."

Remember when I said that I got a strategy back in 2010 to get out of debt? We were $30,000 in debt in December of 2012. God gave me the strategy for *Activate Your Life Calling* and I already had the message, but I needed it formulated in a way to make it available. God gave me the strategy and told me in a dream what to charge, but I had to change my mindset.

My mindset change had to happen because in the dream, I charged people $1,500 to be part of it but I thought, "I do not know if anyone is going to pay $1,500." When I ran a test on it a year before, I charged $25 for four weeks with me and only four people signed up. It was the biggest failure of my first launch.

Then I pulled it back around, listened to God, got the strategy, and made the product three months of very intensive time with me personally and with the private group, for $1,500.

God showed me what to do: a new mentoring message delivered online each week. Participants get exercises to do to activate it. Then the group goes to our private, cutting-edge online community and interacts with others regarding their process. A personal Life Purpose Coach is assigned to them to give feedback and encouragement, and the entire group gives accountability. Once a month I get the entire group together on a 90-minute live breakthrough call.

I took two groups in January of 2013 through *Activate Your Life Calling.* They were thrilled and many of them saw radical changes in their lives. They did not worry about the money or anything like that. Because it was not about the money; it was about helping people. 80% of my ministry offers things either free or at a very low price. Ministry is about helping those in need. But there is also a need to help businesspeople who want to learn Kingdom principles and take their faith to the workplace.

There is something that happens when you pay for something to help you really step up to a higher level. I want you to be able to develop something like this.

There are many people who are critical of those who charge for this kind of service. However, if you look at my ministry model, I have a big funnel opened up and in this big funnel I offer a lot of ministry resources for free: I have *Daily Prophetic Words* for free, I have blogs, I have revelation, I have my monthly webcast that I have been doing for years, and I have free eBooks. We give, give, and give. I give out so much. We have been giving for years and years and years. That is great. But we cannot live on that free model all the time.

We also offer products that I have charged a little less than $10 for. I have audios, eBooks, and printed books. I offer some things that cost under

$100. I have things like the *Dream Crash Course* and different audios and videos that are very affordable. If we were operating in this way in the business world, the charge would be much more. The *Activate Your Life Calling* would actually be more like $5,000 in the business world. Listen to me. This is not about money, but it is about a strategy to help people and expand the Kingdom of God at the same time. I had to change my mindset to do this.

I still give away a ton, but I make available some things like coaching and specialized online webinars, which are focused and extremely affordable. It is part of the giving spirit that is so important.

We are not rich but we are coming to a place where I can now do things that God calls me to do when He calls me to do it. I can give money to missions and people in need. I can free my time to focus on things that matter to God. I was not able to do that before discovering these strategies and renewing my mindset.

ACTIVATION

As we come to the end of this book, I want to pray this activation:

"*Submit to God and be at peace with him; in this way prosperity will come to you. Accept instruction from his mouth and lay up his words in your heart. If you return to the Almighty you will be restored ...*" Job 22:21-23a

As I shared with you previously, we were devastated financially and we trusted God with what He told me to do, and He restored us. God is faithful and if you trust Him, He will restore you as well.

Pray with me:

"Father, I pray right now for the activation. We pray for activation over the callings and the prophetic words that have been given to each of us. I pray for a strategy to get out of debt. I pray for dreams and supernatural experiences. I know that you told me that every time that we share these things that the angelic is activated. The Heavenly realm is activated around this area of breakthrough into something new.

"So, Father, we activate those things. We lay up your words in our heart and we say restore us, Father, into being able to have the finances to change the world and not have the spirit of poverty, or back down in the spirit of fear. I pray for everybody that needs a strategy right now in the name of Jesus, Amen."

The next sections are common questions that I get from people who attend my online training. Be sure to go to the end of this book as I do another activation prayer and tell you more about the many resources I offer.

PART TWO

QUESTIONS & ANSWERS

SEMINAR QUESTIONS

In this section of the book, I will be sharing with you a number of questions and my answers that came up during one of my seminars.

Do you make it a point to sow into areas that you want to see breakthrough in?

Absolutely! Earlier in this book I shared the story of how we got our TV show going and we got back into Hollywood through sowing into that area.

What principles do you use to help you determine where you give your money?

There are so many great causes and many ministries out there that can benefit. How do you choose?

We usually have a foundational place that we tithe to and I do not necessarily lock it all down, but we do have that one place where we tithe. When it comes to giving extra money, nowadays especially, it depends on how God speaks to you.

So what we do is we wait and listen. I remember one time when Linda and I were getting out of debt. We said, "All right God, if you give us extra money, then we will do these different things."

During that time, we got some extra money. We took a percentage of that and just went and blessed people that we would see prophetically.

One day our gardener was outside. I said, "Hey, God told me to give you this." I think it was $100. And he started crying and said, "We could not make our bills this month." Pray. Learn to discern. Ask God. Pace yourself.

Yes, there are a lot of good opportunities. Jesus said that when you sow that some will reap thirty, sixty, or hundredfold (Matthew 13:8) and

I believe that the Kingdom of God really is like that. There are some projects that I call *Kingdom Projects* that God has that will actually benefit more and will bring back more than you initially sowed.

Now, we do not look at it as an investment, but I have noticed that when we sow into things that are cutting edge, that are on God's heart or that are in the community, those things that He speaks to you about, there will be a larger benefit. So ask Him to show you that strategy.

How do you know that you are really helping the needy and giving for a good cause when you sponsor through another ministry? Sometimes people are just plain greedy. You may be hurting instead of helping.

You would have to ask God that. I have never actually thought that. I guess I trust a lot of people. And I know what we do with InLight Connection. We give through our own organization. For example, we directly sponsor one of the kids in World Vision and we give to the Local Food Bank.

We do what we call "$1,000 breakthrough offerings," in which we write a check to the ministries that God speaks to me about. Every time we do this we see something happen in our lives financially. You might want to ask what the money goes to. If it feels like you might have been wounded somewhere in the past with giving, trust that once you give, God is going to give back to you.

I have been a film producer for a Christian movie and have been in the process for five years. I am about to close it down because of the financial problems I am having. Do I stick with the project because I feel like God is calling me to do it, or do I let go of it and move on?

I am not going to give financial advice and I cannot give an exact answer. However, what you need is great discernment here. My sense is that the calling is way bigger than you might realize and you might need to get intercessors in place. You need to get a group praying around you, because if you are called to do something new, you need intense intercession.

Getting intercessors in place is what we are doing right now. When we decided to do our reality show, *The Tattoo Prophet*, we started struggling financially. We had a really, really rough time and we have not been able to do it for two years. I realized there was a lot of resistance against it, and we were going to be doing something new. So, we have to actually gather more intercessors in order to pull things together. We had to get the breakthrough strategy. We even have a paid intercessor on staff!

God is telling me that there are a lot of people who have heard His voice, but have struggled financially. I just released in my prophetic words recently that we are in a time where God is bringing things back around. There were many people ten years ago who were going strong and then everything stopped. For example, in our ministry in 2005, we had a grant for $125,000 and we were going to open a creative coffee house with dream interpretation in Los Angeles. But everything dried up and went the other way.

Now, ten years later, it is coming back around again because everything has shifted. So, just watch and see.

I just want to say God can call you to write a book, produce a movie, or whatever it is that is unique to you. Many times we write it and we just stand back and do not really do anything proactive to promote it or to break through with the book, or the movie in this case. But often there is something proactive we do have to do in order to break through. There is something we must do.

What is your strategy? Perhaps you need to revisit the strategy. When Noah got the strategy to build the ark, he had to swing the hammer. He had to go up against everything there before he could actually do it.

I have written a couple of blogs about developing a breakthrough strategy and I share strategies to get healed and out of debt. You can search these topics on my website and find the blogs.

What is the best way to network job opportunities if you have limited job experience?

The Internet would be one way to do that using networking websites like LinkedIn. But I would say your priority would be to get some experience, even if you have to volunteer. That is what we did.

I had to do this personally. When I was called to go into a computer networking business, I knew some basics but, to be honest with you, I did not know that much about computers. I found someone, (actually the network guy that was coming into the place I worked), and I said to him, "I just want to learn some more stuff; can I tag along with you?"

He agreed. I took a vacation day and went with him on an installation and took notes and offered to work for free. I did that again with a video editing company.

Also, when I wanted to learn more about dreams and dream interpretation, I worked as a volunteer for John Paul Jackson's ministry. I taught myself ColdFusion Programming and served as the webmaster for his ministry.

So, find a place that is doing what you want to do. Read their books. Find out about them and see if you can do some work, some volunteer work, or something to come alongside, because you will need to get some experience, and you will meet people along the way.

God gave my husband and me a non-profit organization but we both have full-time jobs, so we are not sure what to do. How do we do it?

Well, you need to plan. You need to hear the plan of the Lord. He might have given it to you, but is it for now or is it for later? You need to get that strategy; begin to press in.

When I need to hear the Lord, I press in really hard. This is for anybody who needs a breakthrough and needs to hear more clearly. I would start taking communion every day regarding your situation. Also, I often instruct people to pray, "God, show me what Satan does not want me to see," and then pray, "God, show me what is for now and what is for later," and begin to respond based on that.

This is some of the stuff I do with my prophetic life coaching. I usually take 30 minutes to get a breakthrough strategy for an individual. But it is not just hearing God; it is you responding as well. So, pray that God opens your eyes, and opens everything around you so that you will know the answer.

How do you hear a strategy? Because I struggle to hear anything, so how do you know when you are hearing God?

You need to go back to the basics on hearing God and you develop that. The first thing I recommend is to go back to the last time that you remember hearing God. If that has not happened yet, then ask God specifically to speak to you and go back to the last time you heard Him, or you received an answer to prayer and study what it sounded like.

This is how you begin to get used to God's voice. Begin to ask God to speak to you in His word. One of the activation exercises I use with people is to specifically ask God to speak to you through the Bible and do it every day. Ask every day and look up the verses God gives you.

Do not be discouraged if it does not happen right away, because you need to open up your *ears to hear and eyes to see*. This is learning to discern.

Begin to do that and take the time to write down what you hear. Then ask God to speak to you through a movie or the TV or the news. Then ask God to speak to you through a person you know, because you have got to activate those things. Activating the ability to hear God's voice will be the number one strategy for you.

How do you keep your faith in God and His provision rather than in the act of giving? In other words, how do you keep from just doing a method, (like it is magic) versus really having faith in God?

That is a good question. First of all, just rest in the fact that giving is a principle from God. There is something powerful in it and it is a spiritual principle. So just rest in the fact that it is good. This will keep your heart clean.

Usually people pick up guilt in messages they have heard from different people that put them under pressure about giving. However, it does not matter who uses the principle, "If you give, you will receive;" if you just keep your heart right, ask God to bless you and God will bless you.

The reality is that God wants to bless you. These are spiritual principles at work that were designed by God. Sowing and reaping, (or giving and receiving) is a spiritual principle that God initiated and honors.

God responds to our faith and He wants to take care of our needs. We just need to focus our faith in God and His care for us, and then our faith can be released as we follow spiritual principles.

Do not get overly-focused on the process. Trust God and know this: God is going to bless you anyway.

What if you are an entrepreneur and you cannot depend on a regular income? Your income goes up and down month to month, so it is hard to do a regular budget. How do you move forward?

You have got to be careful, budget, and be really disciplined if your income streams fluctuate or are seasonal. I would recommend finding some more income. You do not have to quit what you are doing, but find another way to fill those gaps. That way additional income will shore things up and it will help in the up and down season.

Additionally, pray that God will bring you some type of lump sum, a nest egg, to be able to begin to save. Maybe you could save $100 a month towards that. That would be another good thing. I did this for my taxes as well. Keep in mind that as a contractor you are going to owe taxes. What we did was that every time I would deposit a check that someone would give me, we would transfer 25% of it over to the savings account so that we would have money for taxes right there. You can just do it right away right at the ATM or online, so you will not be tempted later.

My job skills are very limited and I am considering going to college for a degree. Is it ever God's will for you to take out loans and go into debt for college to get a better job?

Well, that is a tough one. It depends if God is calling you to that. There is so much misunderstanding out there and there are so many people taking out these oversized loans when they have not even done the math on if their career is even going to pay it back.

There are calculators out there for that. Maybe you are getting this huge loan for a job as a forest ranger or as a teacher that will not be paid back for 10-20 years. You want to do the math on that and be sure.

I do not know a direct answer. My wife would say never go into debt for anything; just avoid debt at all cost.

But pray about that and see if there are other ways that you can get what you need in order to do what you want to do. Are there other ways to get there?

By the way, getting a degree is not a fix-all, because if you are not already working in that area, even volunteering or something, then you are going to have a real tough time when you graduate. I would recommend getting into that area first and getting some experience, too.

"I have downsized after following Dave Ramsey's advice. I had been in a good situation for a while, and then something happened to me that created huge debt. So, this major event happened and now I am back in debt again and I am discouraged. What do you recommend?"

Well, remember, that all things are possible for those who believe. Begin to pray for God to bring that strategy to get back out. Go back to Dave Ramsey's baby steps, and do whatever you need to do to make some extra money. Do not give up. Seeing that the enemy has hit you twice reveals that there is a calling for you to help others. There is a calling on your life for finances and the enemy is just trying to hold you down. Watch and pray.

"If you fear money and you know that you need money to balance life, how do you deal with that fear?"

If you have fear of money, break it right now. Fear is not of the Lord. *"For God has not given us a spirit of fear, but of power and of love and of a sound mind."* 2 Timothy 1:7 NKJV

Take authority over the spirit of fear. Fear crept in and was accepted after September 11, 2001. Then it crept in even greater after the downturn in 2008. We need to cast out the spirit of fear. It does not belong in your mind. It does not belong in anybody's lives or the Church and the spirit of fear has been driving us for too long. I would begin to pray every day and ask God to remove that spirit of fear and to give you that spirit of boldness to move forward.

"We have been in a legal battle against a big company and we have lost one of them, but the battle is still ongoing. How can we get breakthrough in the legal system, because we feel like we are right?"

You will need a strategy from the Lord, and this is really important because you feel like you are right. I am not saying this is for you, but sometimes you might have to back down from what is right. That is humility. You might have to back down from what is right to be able to get through things.

Now, I am not saying this is specifically for you, but you have to get that wisdom for your situation. Because justice is one thing, and God standing up for the cause of your justice, but you have got to make sure that everything is going to be repaid.

Here is what I have done before. I have taken the humble route because God promised to lift me up in due time, and then it comes back to you in other ways.

"Humble yourselves before the Lord, and he will lift you up." James 4:10

If you are in a lockdown type of situation and it does not seem to be moving, you might want to get that strategy and see if that is it.

I have backed down from things, or we got ripped off in a sense, but then we demanded God's justice to be repaid to us in another way and it worked for us.

God is restoring and bringing justice right now and He will repay you.

"Where do you start to get financial breakthrough when you live paycheck to paycheck? I know you talked a little bit about it with Dave Ramsey. Do you have anything else?"

Try to get extra money. Find a way to get extra money and I am just telling you right now that God has spoken to me that the Internet is a way to break through, or even something locally, and that is the only way.

If you are in a lockdown where you only make so much money and you can only spend so much money, you need to be able to spend less somehow.

I know most people cannot take as radical of a step that I did, but what you can do is make some extra money.

Ask God to show you what it is that you can do to get going on that.

Our small ministry has been financially stressed for eight and a half years. We are cutting back staff, losing staff, trying to raise funds, but nothing is happening. Instead, there has been a lot of healing with the ministry, but no money. We are trying to figure out what God is doing.

Yeah, you need a new strategy. This was us (InLight Connection). Remember the story I shared earlier about reducing our debt?

At that time I was still releasing my prophetic words on ElijahList.com, and doing some of the ministry that I still do.

I was doing everything I knew to do, but we were massively in debt and we could not get out. We were $50,000 in debt at one point in 2008, and then we had gotten it down to $30,000 by 2012. God began to give us a new strategy.

But, I had to change my mindset. I had to get off the road and stop doing some of the things that I did before and ask God for His strategy.

I would go into a time of prayer and seeking the Lord on what your new strategy should be, especially if it has been eight and a half years. Biblically, eight is the number of new beginnings. You have been in this season for eight years and you are moving into nine.

Sometimes you need to re-up at this point and maybe there is some new strategy for healing that is going to come that is going to look totally different. God, we pray that you would reveal strategies right now in Jesus' name.

"I often hear the Lord putting really large numbers on my heart to give to ministries where I attend. But the reality is, I am not sure. I do not want to get into debt giving the money. So how do you do that? How do you sow money into ministry?"

You need to be able to have a balance and know what it is. My wife and I have been givers and givers and givers. I was such a giver for so many years. My heart would be pulled on.

Before I would go into a meeting, I would actually ask God how much I am supposed to give and get it ahead of time. Maybe some of those larger numbers are for later on? It is possible.

Do not go into debt over giving and I have heard a couple of stories where God did something and did a miraculous thing, but that was something that was for a season. It was something the Lord was doing to move things. But overall, you are a giver so you need to listen to the advice I just gave on boundaries and balance and ask God how much you should give. Maybe you could give half or ten percent of what you feel God is saying and then ask Him to increase.

And by the way, I will say this about giving: if you cannot afford 10% that is not a magic number. It is a starting point. I did this years ago. I did not have the money to give that much, so I made a deal with God.

I gave 1-2% and said, "God, I will start doing this and as you give increase I will give more." And sure enough, I began to get raises and other money started coming in.

That is the one thing in Malachi 3; the Lord says to test Him in this.

Are there curses associated with finances? Our family has been struggling with getting out of debt. We are living frugally and just when we are positioned to get out of debt things break, kids get injured. Are there curses?

Absolutely. Those are generational ties to financial losses and things like that. I am remembering Arthur Burk has an audio teaching on seven curses. It is an amazing teaching on recognizing and breaking repeated patterns that block your blessings.

When I listened to his message, I discovered certain curses that needed to be broken. I did not even know those existed until he showed me. He actually laid out the symptoms and we prayed and broke it and things turned around.

So, yes, there are curses and you want to identify them. And again, pray that prayer that the Lord will show you what Satan does not want you to see. Do it every day. I do communion every single day and I am praying those types of prayers and responding to what God shows me.

How do people get a breakthrough when they have been stuck in a rut for a really long time? What do they do?

You can do some of the steps I have been talking about here and come into agreement with someone. Really come into agreement. Get someone to agree with you in prayer.

Usually someone that is stuck almost always has a negative atmosphere around them. Everything you say bounces off them, such as "I cannot get anyone; there is no one to pray." It does not matter! Do you want to be stuck? Ask God for someone.

I am not trying to be mean. I am trying to say you need some spiritual plastic explosives around you right now to get this thing unstuck.

Take a step. I started taking communion every single day. I started doing this when I was sick; I have gotten healed over the last month.

I suffered for two years, but I did not fall into the sickness; I fell back on the Lord. I began to pray and take communion every single day. Every single day find someone to come into agreement with you. Begin to ask God to show you what the enemy does not want you to see and then take steps forward.

I was given a word last week that I will have a ministry in life coaching, but I do not have any experience in that. How do I get experience in coaching?

Well, first of all prophetic words could be for down the road to prepare you right now. So you do not want to go out and sell everything based on a prophetic word without having something in place. You want to be careful and move your way into it.

You know, people ask me all the time about how I became a life coach. I am the kind of person who is self-taught. I went through a coaching certification. My coaching training was more of a secular model, which I would not necessarily recommend for anyone else. I would recommend Christian coach training. There are many of them out there. I know that Bethel Church in Redding, California offers that kind of training.

Just so you know, even if you become a coach, even if you become a certified Life Coach, it does not mean you are going to have money. You still have to learn to market. You still have to get clients and find a way to do it or find a niche in it.

But here is the thing, if you feel called to coaching or you have gotten a word, it could be that you actually are a coach. You have this gift. People open their problems up to you all the time, because they feel comfortable. It is like having a pastoral calling or anointing without being a pastor. You have this ability to help people. So ask God to open it up for you.

As part of my *Activate Your Life Calling* course I give a life purpose coaching tool kit at the end of the session that many people have been using with others. You would get this after you go through the 12 weeks. And then you can use the life purpose toolkit to help others with their breakthrough process. As you help others, you get your breakthrough as well.

PERSONAL NOTES
AND GOALS

_____

_____

_____

_____

_____

_____

_____

_____

_____

_____

_____

_____

_____

_____

_____

_____

_____

_____

CLOSING

Thank you for taking time to read this book. As we close, I want to pray for a breakthrough for your life and success. We are going to a new level, and we just want to bless you, the reader, and bless what you are doing right now.

"Father, I pray for a breakthrough. I pray for open doors, dreams and visions. I pray God, that as we move into this new season that there is a shifting in the atmosphere. We break off all the negative prophecies. We pray in Jesus' name.

"God is saying He has shifted the timetable prophetically. Many prophets have not caught it yet, but we are now in a whole new timetable. I hear the Lord saying to plan long, get ready. Do not pull back. This is a time to move forward. Amen."

Please stay in touch with me through my website or on social media. If this book has helped you or you get a breakthrough from what you learned here, please reach out to me on Facebook or Twitter and let me and others know. There is power in sharing your testimony and it will encourage others as well.

ABOUT DOUG

Doug Addison is a prophetic dream interpreter, speaker, writer, Life Coach, and stand-up comedian. Doug travels the world bringing a message of love, hope, and having fun! His unique style helps open people to discover their destiny and experience God's supernatural love and power. Doug releases *Daily Prophetic Words* and is the author of *Understand Your Dreams Now: Spiritual Dream Interpretation* and *Personal Development God's Way.* He and his wife Linda live in Los Angeles, California.

DougAddison.com

OTHER RESOURCES FROM DOUG ADDISON

UNDERSTAND YOUR DREAMS NOW: SPIRITUAL DREAM INTERPRETATION

Doug Addison's *Understand Your Dreams Now: Spiritual Dream Interpretation* is drawn from decades of classroom and real-world experiences. It contains everything you need to get started or to go to a new level of interpreting dreams. Includes a 300-symbol dream dictionary.

PERSONAL DEVELOPMENT GOD'S WAY

People everywhere want to know their life's purpose and destiny. *Personal Development God's Way* was developed after Doug Addison spent a lifetime studying why some people's lives change radically and others do not. Packed full of practical examples, stories, and exercises designed to apply to your life.

ACCELERATING INTO YOUR LIFE'S PURPOSE

Discover your destiny, awaken passion, and transform your life with this ten-day interactive program. Designed to reveal your life's desires, remove obstacles, and create a written plan for what to focus on next. Change limiting beliefs, stop the past from affecting your future and develop a strategy to guide you towards your destiny. Includes ten audios & transformation journal.

SPIRITUAL IDENTITY THEFT EXPOSED

The rise of identity theft in the world today parallels what is happening spiritually to people everywhere.

People have been blinded to their true identity and the destiny they were created to live. *Spiritual Identify Theft Exposed* contains seven strategies from darkness and seven remedies to change your life forever.

WRITE A BOOK QUICKLY: UNLOCK YOUR CREATIVE SPIRIT

Whether you are just starting out or are an experienced writer, this precise book can help you get to a new level. Tap into your creative nature, learn secrets of writing, publishing tips, writing resources, exercises, and more.

DREAM CRASH COURSE ONLINE TRAINING

Understanding dreams does not have to be difficult! Doug Addison is an expert dream interpreter who has interpreted over 25,000 dreams and has trained thousands of dream interpreters worldwide. He has developed a "crash course" on how to understand your dreams quickly. This is everything you need in one online program. Includes ten online videos,

MP3s, study guide, dream journal, symbols dictionary and more!

PROPHETIC TATTOO & PIERCING INTERPRETATION ONLINE TRAINING

Now you can learn the inside secrets to Prophetic Tattoo and Piercing Interpretation from Doug Addison.

After years of development, Doug Addison is making this one-of-a-kind online training available to you, but only for a short while. Find what you need to get started in this new cutting-edge outreach strategy!

Includes seven online videos, MP3s, study guide, tattoo reference cards, and more.

PROPHETIC LIFE COACHING

Doug Addison is a certified Life Coach and a gifted prophetic strategist. A session with his unique expertise can help with your personal life, business, family, health, relationships, personal development, and even understanding your dreams.

Doug's coaching strategies help people in all areas of life. Prophetic Life Coaching can help you break through the common barriers that people experience in finding and fulfilling their destiny.

In your one-to-one telephone session, Doug helps direct you toward your divine life purpose by evaluating your current situation, getting deeper spiritual insight, and identifying obstacles.

ACTIVATE YOUR LIFE CALLING ONLINE COMMUNITY

Are you ready to bring lasting change in your life, now? Do you want to discover and fulfill your higher calling? Do you want passion to get up each day knowing you are working towards your purpose?

Join us during this three-month interactive program to *Activate Your Life Calling.* This online coaching group is designed to bring the transformation in your life that you have always desired, whether that is helping you lose weight, getting a better job, launching a business or ministry, writing a book, or deepening your relationship with God ... we provide all the support, practice, and feedback you need to break through quickly! *Activate Your Life Calling* will give you all the tools you need to succeed! See you there!

Visit: dougaddison.com/store

Made in the USA
San Bernardino, CA
14 May 2016